Did Yo
LIVERI
THE WIRRAL

A MISCELLANY

Compiled by Julia Skinner
With particular reference to the work of Cliff Hayes

THE FRANCIS FRITH COLLECTION

www.francisfrith.com

Based on a book first published in the United Kingdom in 2006 by The Francis Frith Collection®

Hardback edition published in 2009 ISBN 978-1-84589-415-3

British Library Cataloguing in Publication Data

Did You Know? Liverpool and the Wirral - A Miscellany
Compiled by Julia Skinner
With particular reference to the work of Cliff Hayes

The Francis Frith Collection
Frith's Barn, Teffont,
Salisbury, Wiltshire SP3 5QP
Tel: +44 (0) 1722 716 376
Email: info@francisfrith.co.uk
www.francisfrith.com

Printed and bound in Singapore

Front Cover: **LIVERPOOL, THE EXCHANGE 1887** 20001p

The colour-tinting is for illustrative purposes only, and is not intended to be historically accurate

CONTENTS

INTRODUCTION

'Gateway to the British Empire', 'Second City in England', 'Door to the New World'- all these titles have been used to describe the city of Liverpool. By the start of the 20th century Liverpool had built itself up into a world-class city with seven miles of docks full of ocean-going ships. Shipping companies built citadels that matched their world status, and insurance companies, whose fortunes waxed or waned with the fortunes of those shipping companies, vied with each other to build the grandest offices in the city centre.

Upwards of 200 ships once left Liverpool every week for each corner of the British empire, and indeed the world. Ships went to Canada for corn, and carried iron goods to South America and Africa, and railway carriages to Brazil and South Africa. Ships loaded with generators and electrical goods for Australia and New Zealand brought wool and mutton back. India, China and Japan, Egypt - everywhere on the globe was once covered by ships from Liverpool. Over the years much of this shipping trade has gone, and the riverfront is less busy. Containerisation, mechanisation, in fact a whole new world is now taking over; but instead of going into a decline, Liverpool is once more thriving in a different way and rising to new challenges that lie ahead. Liverpool today is one of the country's most successful and promising cities.

Over the water is the Wirral peninsula, where long stretches of sandy coastline and holiday resorts lie close to the cranes, grain elevators and oil-refinery tanks of Ellesmere Port and Birkenhead. Ellesmere Port developed and prospered with the opening of the Manchester Ship Canal, whilst Birkenhead, the largest town on the Wirral, was the dream of one man, John Laird. In about 1824 he came to a small hamlet of a few hundred people, started his shipbuilding firm, and set about planning a town. Because it was all laid out at the same time, Birkenhead was very neat and orderly. It did have areas of back-to-back houses for the newly imported workers, but there were never the slums of the older towns and cities. Soon Birkenhead became a town, and was granted its Charter of Incorporation in 1877.

To the west of the Wirral is the lovely River Dee, with its expansive estuary that is so important to the wildlife in the area; to the east is the mighty River Mersey, with its docks and factories; and to the north is that part of the Irish Sea known as Liverpool Bay. All have played a massive part in the region's past and present, and no doubt will play a part in its future.

The story of this historic area is full of colourful characters and events, of which this book can only provide a brief glimpse.

BIRKENHEAD, THE DOCKS c1965 B399091

LOCAL DIALECT WORDS AND PHRASES

'Ackers' - money.

'Jigger' - a narrow passage between houses.

'Delf' - crockery.

'Neshed' - feeling very cold.

'You're in Dicky's meadow' - You're in real trouble.

'Ollies' - marbles.

'Welt' - a tea break.

'Antwacky' - old fashioned, out of date.

'Jangle' - a good gossip.

'Woolyback' - a non-Liverpudlian.

'Scouser' - this well-known nickname for anyone from Liverpool originates from a sort of stew popular in the Merseyside area known as Lobscouse, shortened to Scouse. The dish and its name were probably derived from a north German stew called Labskaus, which was popular with seafarers in the 18th and 19th centuries. A recipe for Scouse is given on page 46.

'Plastic Scouser' - a term used to describe a person who sounds Scouse but does not come from Liverpool. Often used to refer to people in Birkenhead and Wallasey.

HAUNTED LIVERPOOL AND THE WIRRAL

Mysterious activity at Liverpool Playhouse frightened workmen in 1999 when the building was being renovated. Strange incidents that were reported included taps being switched on when no one was there, a feeling of a strange presence in the basement, and doors suddenly slamming shut which were so heavy that they were usually difficult to open and close. The Playhouse is said to be haunted by the ghost of a former cleaner named Elizabeth, who was killed in 1897 whilst she was cleaning the stage; the fire iron came down and struck her, causing her to fall into the orchestra pit, breaking her neck in the process. Her death was recorded as an accident, but as the fire iron at that time was water powered and needed someone to operate it, she may in fact have been murdered. Elizabeth's ghost is said to haunt the theatre's gallery level, and was last seen in 1996. The haunting is especially linked with the seat A5, which is said to always be cold. Two other ghosts are said to roam the Playhouse. One is the Grey Lady, a woman wearing a grey coat and hood who wanders around the stalls, and the other is a man dressed in a frock coat and top hat who also haunts the area of the stalls and the coffee bar - he is said to be searching for his daughter, who ran away to join a theatre company in the early 1900s.

Liverpool's Royal Court Theatre is said to be haunted by the ghost of a man known as Les. He is believed to have been a caretaker at the theatre who died of exposure after slipping and breaking his leg whilst working on the roof on a cold winter's day.

Rocky's Nightclub at Birkenhead has a resident ghost which has been seen many times in recent years, and is said to have frightened some members of staff to the extent that they have left their jobs. The ghost is of a young man who appears to be wearing boxing gloves; the story is that the premises used to be a boxing club, and the man died there after his first fight. The ghost has been given the name of 'Knocker' because of his habit of knocking over glasses in the bar as well as knocking on doors, and is said to have knocked against members of staff as well.

The ghost of Old Mother Redcap is said to haunt the area around her old inn (now demolished) at Egremont, near New Brighton, looking for the sailors' gold that she hid away for safe-keeping (and see pages 36-37).

LIVERPOOL AND THE WIRRAL MISCELLANY

The balcony of Liverpool's Town (now City) Hall has seen some of Liverpool's most memorable moments. Both Everton and Liverpool Football Clubs have waved to the crowds from here. The Beatles stood there in the late 1960s on their last combined visit to Liverpool, attracting a crowd of 100,000 in Castle Street. The figure on the roof is often wrongly identified as Britannia, but is actually Minerva, goddess of the sea and keeper of wisdom.

In 1872 the Reverend Francis Kilvert described the scene on the Mersey: "The Mersey was gay and almost crowded with vessels of all sorts moving up and down the river, ships, barques, brigs, brigantines, schooners, cutters, colliers, tugs, steamboats, lighters, 'flats', everything from the huge emigrant liner steamship with four masts to the tiny sailing and rowing boat. From the river one sees to advantage the miles of docks which line the Mersey side, and the forests of masts which crowd the quays, 'the pine forest of the sea, and spar' … Nothing gives one so vivid an idea of the vast commerce of the country as these docks, quays and immense warehouses, piled and cumbered with hides, cotton, tallow, corn, oilcake, wood and wine, oranges and other fruit and merchandise of all kinds from all corners of the world."

The Liverpool & Manchester Railway opened in 1830 and was the world's first commercially successful line. It was built by George Stephenson (1781-1848), whose locomotive 'Rocket' heralded the railway age.

LIVERPOOL, THE TOWN HALL 1895 36650

LIVERPOOL, THE ADELPHI HOTEL 1870 7841

Photograph 7841 (above) shows the original Adelphi Hotel, which was built c1840 on the site of the Adelphi Gardens by the Midland Railway Company. This building was demolished in 1912 and the present Adelphi Hotel was built on the same site, with its architecture based on the style of an Atlantic liner.

Liverpool was born thanks to a charter from King John in 1207. He promised land and equality to all who moved there, and thus the wonderful mix that makes up the people of Liverpool was started. It is thought that the king wanted a port in the district that was free from the control of the Earl of Chester.

St George's Hall was started in 1838 to accommodate the Liverpool Music Festival, and is one of the most impressive buildings in England. The designer, Harvey Longsdale Elmes, was only 23 when he won two design competitions, firstly for the Music Hall and then for new Law Courts for Liverpool, and put the two buildings into one. Because of the change of plans and uses of the hall, building work did not start in earnest until 1842. Sadly, Elmes never saw his magnificent work completed. The extra work put such a strain on him that he fell ill, and was sent on a sea journey to recuperate. He died just after arriving in Jamaica, and was laid to rest there. His work was taken over by C R Cockerell, and the hall was opened in 1854. It is a strange mixture - concert hall, law courts, theatre, cells and jail - but it works well and remains a marvellous and unique building.

LIVERPOOL, ST GEORGE'S HALL c1881 7813

LIVERPOOL, THE MERSEY FERRY BOATS c1965 L60021

NEW BRIGHTON, THE BEACH 1887 20067

Today ferries from Liverpool only ply to Birkenhead and Seacombe, but at one time there were ferries across the Mersey to New Brighton, Egremont, Seacombe, Birkenhead, Rock Ferry and Eastham; before the Mersey Tunnel opened, vehicle ferries also ran to Seacombe and Birkenhead. Photograph L60021 (opposite) shows the Wallasey diesel ferries 'Egremont' (leaving for New Brighton) and 'Leasowe' (for Seacombe). The ferry in the background is one of Birkenhead's diesel ferries.

New Brighton was developed from open waste space, and was laid out specifically to be an attraction. James Atherton was the man with the dream, helped and supported by John Askew. Although the original plans were very grand and exciting, money proved a problem. Costs kept on rising before income started to come in, and the large mansions that were planned became ordinary houses, and the exclusive hotels became boarding houses and cafés. Also known as Perch Rock and the Battery, the Fort was, and still is, a very large landmark on the New Brighton shore, and can be seen in photograph 20067, opposite. Completed in 1825 at a cost of £25,000, it was part of the defences on the River Mersey, and was used to store gunpowder for ships visiting Liverpool. It is now used as a museum.

The Mersey ferries were made famous by the song "Ferry 'Cross the Mersey" by Gerry and the Pacemakers. The song is now played on the ferryboats themselves every time they prepare to dock at Liverpool.

LIVERPOOL, THE LONDON & NORTH WESTERN RAILWAY HOTEL 1890 26662

The London & North Western Railway Hotel (photograph 26662, above) stands on St George's Plateau. It was built by the London & North Western Railway Company, and opened in 1871, with 330 rooms. The corporation felt so strongly that development around St George's Plateau should complement the grandeur of St George's Hall that they paid towards the cost of the Storeton stone from the Wirral for this Renaissance-style building. Today, after standing empty for many years, the building is owned by the John Moores University, and is used as student accommodation.

The Walker Art Gallery in Liverpool (photograph 36647, below) was opened in 1877. The bas-relief friezes along the front of the building represent four royal visits to Liverpool: from right to left, beginning in Mill Lane, they show the embarkation of William III and his army at Hoylake in 1690; continuing in William Brown Street are King John granting the first charter to the burgesses of Liverpool in 1207; the visit of Queen Victoria in 1851; and the laying of the foundation stone of the Walker Art Gallery by the Duke of Edinburgh in 1874. On the roof over the main entrance to the Gallery is an allegorical statue of Liverpool, by John Warrington Wood. The large female figure in Carrara marble is seated on a bale of cotton, crowned with a laurel wreath, and holding a trident in one hand, and a ship's propeller in the other. The Walker Art Gallery houses an outstanding art collection, including the famous 'And When Did You Last See Your Father?' by WF Yeames.

LIVERPOOL, THE WALKER ART GALLERY 1895 36647

An Eiffel-style Tower at New Brighton was always part of the original dream of James Atherton as he planned his new holiday resort. It was started in 1896 and opened in 1898. At 631ft high, it was the tallest structure in England at the time (see photograph 45163, opposite). Sadly, money was short, and maintenance was haphazard. During the First World War the tower was allowed to rot, and in 1918 it was declared unsafe. No money could be found to repair the tower, so in 1919 work started on dismantling it. By Easter 1921 it was gone. The building below the tower lasted until it was destroyed by fire in 1969.

Liverpool Castle was probably erected in the 1230s. The castle was ruined during the Civil War and completely demolished in the 18th century. The site of the castle was at the present-day Derby Square, near the city centre, where the modern-day law courts were built in the style of a castle.

In the 19th century the rivalry between Liverpool and Manchester was such that advisors to Queen Victoria said that the honour of the title of Lord Mayor could not be given to the mayor of one city and not the other. At exactly 11am on 3 August 1893, one of Queen Victoria's ministers entered the office of both Liverpool's and Manchester's mayor and laid before each Her Majesty's permission to use the title of Lord Mayor; thus neither could claim a victory over the other.

NEW BRIGHTON, THE TOWER AND THE SANDS 1900 45163

LIVERPOOL, THE CUSTOM HOUSE 1887 20015

Photograph 20015, above, shows Liverpool's fifth Customs & Excise collection building, which was built in the 1820s. Collecting tolls and excise duty was an important business, which demanded an important building, but sadly this lovely structure was destroyed in the blitz of the Second World War.

The Great Famine in Ireland in the 1840s meant that Irish people left their homeland in their thousands in search of a better life. Many of them came to Liverpool, some to join ships that would take them to America and Australia, but others to settle. By 1851, approximately 25% of the population of Liverpool was Irish-born.

St Peter's was the name of the church shown in photograph 26665 (below), which gave Church Street its name. Liverpool was given parish status in 1699; plans were made to build a new church for the parish, which had broken away from Walton. St Nicholas's Church was already there, but it was looked upon as a seamen's church and a church for the merchants, so St Peter's was built in 1704 for the citizens, paid for with money that was raised by pre-selling the pews and boxes in the church to the better-off families of Liverpool. After Liverpool became a city in 1880, St Peter's was used as a cathedral whilst a new, grander building was planned. St Peter's Church was pulled down in the early 1920s.

LIVERPOOL, THE PRO-CATHEDRAL (ST PETER'S CHURCH) 1890 26665

BIRKENHEAD, THE CROSSROADS 1954 B399006

BIRKENHEAD, CHARING CROSS 1967 B399044

Liverpool has two famous modern cathedrals. The Anglican Liverpool Cathedral, begun in 1904 by Giles Gilbert Scott and finished in 1978, is built of red sandstone in Gothic style. Its aisles are unusual in being built as tunnels through the walls. The Roman Catholic Metropolitan Cathedral was designed by Sir Frederick Gibberd and consecrated in 1967. The building was originally designed by Sir Edward Lutyens as a huge Classical-style dome, but the Second World War and soaring costs dictated the change of plan to a more contemporary design. It features glass designed by John Piper and Patrick Reyntiens.

Adolf Hitler's half-brother Alois and his Irish sister-in-law Bridget Dowling are known to have lived in Upper Stanhope Street in Liverpool in the early years of the 20th century. In the 1970s Bridget's alleged memoirs were found which said that Adolf himself stayed with them in the city in 1912-1913, but the memoirs are now widely believed to be a forgery.

It is no exaggeration to say that many of the grand buildings which grace Liverpool's skyline and waterfront are founded on the financial gains from slavery. The city's entrepreneurs embraced the slave trade wholeheartedly, prospering in the operation of the system known as 'triangular trading': cotton textiles and manufactured goods were sent to West Africa to be exchanged for slaves, who were in turn taken to the southern states of America and the West Indies, to be exchanged again for sugar, alcohol, tobacco and raw cotton. In one of the busiest years, 1798, 149 Liverpool slaving vessels carried a total of 53,051 slaves, and by the end of the 18th century Liverpool had eclipsed both Bristol and London to become the country's main slave port. Slavery became illegal in the British Empire in 1834, but many poignant reminders of the slave trade can still be seen around Liverpool, such as the carved African heads on the City Hall.

ELLESMERE PORT, THE MANCHESTER SHIP CANAL 1947 M340501

During the Second World War there were 80 air raids on Merseyside; an especially heavy series of raids in May 1941 interrupted operations at the docks for almost a week. 2,500 people were killed, almost half the homes in the metropolitan area sustained some damage and 11,000 were totally destroyed. The Beatle John Lennon was born in Liverpool during an air raid on 9 October 1940.

The Waterloo Column at the top of Liverpool's William Brown Street, on Commutation Row, is the city's version of Nelson's Column in London (see photograph 36645 on page 45). On it stands a statue of Arthur Wellesley, 1st Duke of Wellington, British general, statesman and Prime Minister. He is commemorated here as the victorious leader of the British forces in the Peninsular War 1808-14, and the final victory against Napoleon at the Battle of Waterloo in 1815. The column stands 132ft high, and the Duke's statue adds a further 15ft. It is said that the statue was forged using metal from cannon captured at the Battle of Waterloo.

In September 1928, Liverpool was officially 'married to the sea' as part of the celebrations of Civic Week. The idea was inspired by an old custom from Venice. From a platform overhanging the River Mersey, surrounded by dignitaries and a choir of 300 children, Sir Archibald Savidge gave a speech outlining how the sea had been the reason that Liverpool had grown from a tiny fishing village to a port of world-wide importance. He also noted that the city wins its bread from the waters and has overcome fast tides and natural difficulties. He then threw a ring into the sea as a token of the partnership between the city and the sea. The ring is still down there to this day, buried in the silt at the bottom of the Mersey.

LIVERPOOL, THE EXCHANGE 1895 36655

LIVERPOOL, THE OVERHEAD RAILWAY 1895 36658

The Exchange building seen in photograph 36655, opposite, opened in 1808. The area in front was known as Exchange Flags, and much of the shipping and insurance business of Liverpool was done on this square behind the Town Hall. In the middle of the Flags stands the monument erected to commemorate Lord Nelson. The monument has four grilles, which provide air vents for what was once a tobacco warehouse underneath it. Also under part of the Flags is the secret bunker where operations for the North Atlantic were masterminded during the Second World War.

The Royal Navy once had much stronger links with Liverpool than it does now. Quite often the whole of the Channel Fleet would exercise in the Irish Sea, and then have a three- or four-day visit to Liverpool, to show the merchants and people of the city that the Navy had the power and might to look after the Merchant Fleet.

Photograph 36658, opposite, shows Liverpool's Overhead Railway, which ran from north to south in the city and yet did not hold up traffic going down to the Pier Head. It was the first elevated electric railway in Britain to have automatic signalling, and there were many other 'firsts' for this private venture. It was initially opposed by the City Council and by the Docks & Harbour Board, both of which it served well for almost a century. The large ornate wooden Pier Head Station can be seen on the right of the photograph.

LIVERPOOL, THE FLOATING ROAD 1895 36660

Liverpool's Floating Road can be seen in photograph 36660, above, which was taken from the Prince's Landing Stage looking up the floating road towards St Nicholas's Place. The floating road was supported on pontoons that rose and fell with the tide, which is high in the photograph. This meant that wagons and horses could drive straight on to the landing stage and board the luggage ferries for the journey across the Mersey, whatever the state of the tide.

Liverpool is famous the world over as the home of the Beatles, but the Cavern Club in Mathew Street where the Fab Four performed has now been demolished. There is a replica of the Cavern Club in The Beatles Story, a visitor attraction on Albert Dock.

The White Star line started in Liverpool when Thomas Henry Ismay bought a bankrupt shipping company in 1868. He put money, new ships and new life into the company, and brought in the right partners and associates to found the successful business. White Star, whose motto was 'Ready and Steadfast', always aimed at the best. The SS 'Adriatic', seen in photograph 24417, below, was built in 1872 and was the fifth of the company's liners. Not a lucky ship, she collided with Cunard's 'Parthia' at New York in October 1875, and in December the same year she hit the sailing ship 'Harvest Queen', drowning all on board. Her speed and metal bows got her into trouble again in July 1885, when she sank the brigantine 'G A Pink' - five crew died. Laid up in Birkenhead in 1890, she was taken to Preston for breaking up in 1899.

LIVERPOOL, HMS 'ADRIATIC' 1890 24417

BIRKENHEAD, THE QUEENSWAY TUNNEL c1965 B399027

BIRKENHEAD, THE DOCKS c1965 B399036

The Queensway Tunnel was opened by George V and Queen Mary on 18 July 1934 and was the first of the two road traffic tunnels to be dug under the Mersey; it soon replaced the car ferries and luggage boats. Some 200,000 people gathered to watch the event, and 80,000 of those celebrated with a 'tunnel walk' through from Liverpool to Birkenhead. On the Birkenhead side, to create the large tunnel entrance and the lead-up area, many back-to-back houses had to be pulled down; the town's library also had to be demolished, but the biggest job was moving the gas mains and sewers.

Birkenhead Docks were started on 23 October 1844, when the foundation stone was laid. Before that, ships sheltered or tied up in Bidston Pool, which lay between Birkenhead and Seacombe. John Laird (son of William Laird who built the first shipbuilding yard at Wallasey) started his shipbuilding business in Bidston Pool; he moved to the Mersey when the dock building began there. The Birkenhead Docks were once an independent company, but money troubles forced them to join the Mersey Docks & Harbour Board and to be controlled from Liverpool. The arrival of the railway in the 1840s made the need for deep water docks even more essential. The Great Western Railway ran into Birkenhead and the Docks, and the London Midland Scottish Railway ran into Liverpool.

Birkenhead contains the oldest standing building on Merseyside - Birkenhead Priory, whose Benedictine monks were granted a charter around 1150 to run the first ferry across the River Mersey.

Birkenhead's Great Float Dock provided employment directly and indirectly for over 100 years before competition from Europe and improvements in road transport sent it into decline. In recent years substantial government and private funding has been invested in Birkenhead; the land at the eastern end of the Great Float has been developed as the Twelve Quays, and the port is now the terminal for cargo and passenger services between Merseyside and Ireland. A floating stage can work with two roll-on/roll-off ferries at the same time. The ferries can save an hour on an Irish Sea crossing as they no longer have to travel through Liverpool's enclosed dock system.

Photograph E9031, opposite, shows the old village centre of Eastham, with its unusual war memorial and village cross, and the massively buttressed tower of the parish church. Among the gravestones in the churchyard are those of many young men who perished learning to fly at the nearby Hooton Air Strip. Philip Thickness, the man who designed the Cunard Building in Liverpool, also lies here.

Ellesmere Port was created when the Earl of Ellesmere constructed a canal from Ellesmere in Shropshire to meet the River Mersey, to bring goods from the Potteries to Liverpool for world-wide distribution. The small village of Whitby, where the canal met the river, was renamed Ellesmere Port. Photograph E135009, opposite, shows the docks that linked the Ellesmere Canal (now called the Shropshire Union Canal) with the Manchester Ship Canal, with tall flour mills in the background.

EASTHAM, STANLEY LANE c1965 E9031

ELLESMERE PORT, FLOUR MILLS AND THE DOCKS c1955 E135009

Work began on the Manchester Ship Canal in 1887. However, only 15,870 of the navvies who built it were able to clock off at the end of their final shift: 130 lost their lives during the construction of the Canal, and countless others lost fingers, hands, toes, feet and whole limbs in the harsh and dangerous working conditions that prevailed. When it opened in 1894 the Ship Canal gave countless industries on the Mersey a chance to import and export more cheaply and easily. Ellesmere Port was a favourite dock for timber from Russia and Scandinavia, which was moved from here all over the north for house building. The 35-mile-long Manchester Ship Canal works as one great harbour, and ships moving up and down the canal have to register each movement with the control centre at Eastham.

Though fishing was the principal industry of the village of Wallasey, James Stonehouse, who knew the area in the late 17th century, portrayed the inhabitants as a shifty lot who made their real livings through less legal means. He wrote that 'the inhabitants were nearly all wreckers and smugglers - they ostensibly carried on the trade and calling of fishermen, farm-labourers and small farmers; but they were deeply saturated with the sins of covetousness, and many a fierce fire has been lighted on the Wirral shore on stormy nights to lure the good ships on the Burbo or Hoyle Banks. There is scarcely a house in the north Wirral that could not provide a guest with a good stiff glass of brandy or Hollands.' Perhaps that explains why it was said that the flames had the blue haze of burning brandy on one of the occasions when St Hilary's Church at Wallasey burnt down!

BIRKENHEAD, WOODCHURCH ROAD, PRENTON 1954 B399002

BIRKENHEAD, HAMILTON SQUARE 1967 B399039

UPTON, THE VILLAGE c1960 U36013

Upton is an ancient Viking village just three miles from the Irish Sea, now almost entirely overtaken by the encroachments of Birkenhead. Its 19th-century church has a 1,000-year-old Viking runic stone in a showcase.

The village of Thornton Hough on the Wirral has an unusual church clock, which has five clock faces. The church was built by a retired Yorkshire woollen manufacturer, Joseph Hirst, who lived at Thornton House. He had a clock face put on all four sides of the church tower, but then found that he could not see the clock from his house, because of an intervening wall. He solved the problem by adding a fifth clock face higher up on one side, so that he could see it from home.

Liverpool will hold the European Capital of Culture title in 2008. This announcement in 2003 prompted a £750 million regeneration of part of the city centre.

As oil tankers increased in size in the 1950s some of them were difficult to handle on the Manchester Ship Canal. Eastham Oil Dock was constructed in 1954 to allow these larger tankers to discharge their cargoes without entering the Ship Canal. It was built on the landward side of the canal so that its pipes and equipment did not have to pass over or under the Manchester Ship Canal. As can be seen in photograph E9504 (below), the entrance is right next to the Ship Canal entrance lock. The top ship in the photograph is in the Ship Canal lock, the other three are in Eastham Dock.

EASTHAM, THE DOCK c1965 E9504

WALLASEY, THE CHURCH AND THE TOWER c1873 8468

The old Wirral village of Wallasey has developed slowly, and even today there are still some of the older buildings dotted around. The Wirral was colonised by Norsemen long ago, and many names reflect those invaders who settled here - Wallasey means 'the low land (or island) where the Welsh live'. St Hilary's is the old parish church of Wallasey, seen in photograph 8468, above. There are not many churches dedicated to this saint, and this particular church is unique because of its two towers. There has been a church on this site for over a thousand years. A fire has twice destroyed the buildings: the lone tower dates from a church built in or around 1530, which caught fire in the 1850s. The tower was saved, and the new church, seen behind, was built slightly away from the old tower. The older tower is noted for its gargoyles.

Wallasey Docks were built on what was known as Wallasey Pool, a once wild and beautiful tidal creek. The first boilermaking and shipbuilding yard was established by William Laird in the mid 1820s. In 1829 William Laird launched his first iron ship, a 60-ton lighter for use in Ireland. Dock development in Wallasey Pool continued at a pace from then on, with Egerton and Morpeth Docks opening in 1847, Alfred Dock being finished in 1851 and Wallasey Dock opening in 1877. From 1945 the number of people employed by the shipbuilding yards in Wallasey and Birkenhead declined and a number of associated industries closed. To offset this, other trades began to expand and diversify, and new factories opened. Wallasey Docks became the main grain importing area for Merseyside. The Homepride Flour Mills can be seen in photograph W164088, below, and the vessel on the left of the photograph is a cargo boat registered in Karachi, probably delivering grain from Asia.

WALLASEY, THE DOCKS c1965 W164088

Egremont was never as commercial as its sister New Brighton,
but it was still a popular holiday destination. The black and
white timber building on the left of photograph 36685, below,
was Old Mother Redcap's Inn, which was steeped in history,
with stories of shipwrecks, sailors' gold and smugglers. The inn
was popular with sailors and smugglers, who left their pay and

prize money with Mother Redcap for her to keep safe in various hiding places. After Mother Redcap's death very little money or gold was found in the inn; local tradition says that there is still gold buried somewhere in this area, and that one day a large hidden cache of treasure may well be found! The inn was pulled down in the 1970s.

EGREMONT, FROM THE SANDS 1895 36685

PORT SUNLIGHT, CHRIST CHURCH c1960 P188053

EGREMONT THE LANDING STAGE 1890 24427

Port Sunlight was the dream of William Lever, a man who believed that there was good in everyone; only the best would do for his workers and employees. He moved his soap-making factory from Warrington to Bromborough Dock around 1888, and then set about building homes for the workers. The estate covered 770 acres, including the works, and when it was finished, it housed around 6,000 people. Every cottage was said to be different, and an assortment of architects was employed to help turn a swampy muddy creek into a wonderful Garden Village. Lever, later Lord Leverhulme, added every amenity he could think of to the village: a clubhouse, library, hospital, gymnasium and swimming baths were all included. The building Lord Leverhulme was said to be proudest of was Christ Church, the place of worship that he built in Port Sunlight (photograph P188053, opposite). It looks much older than the century in which it was built, and has a very solid yet charming feel to it.

The landing stage at Egremont seen in photograph 24427, opposite, was built to replace an original from 1835; it lasted until 1909, when it was replaced. When a tanker hit the pier in May 1932, it took a year to repair it; there was no hurry, because the Seacombe pier could be used - the passengers would go the last mile by bus. In 1940, during war-time blackouts, the pier was hit again, very badly, by a ship ready to form a convoy to cross the North Atlantic. This time the pier was abandoned, and before the war was over, it had disappeared completely.

Liverpool's Italian population lived mainly in Gerard, Hunter, Lionel and Whale Streets, off Scotland Road, causing the area to be known as 'Little Italy'.

Tradition says that a lighthouse was built on the sands at New Brighton in the early 1700s, but it collapsed into the sand. A ship carrying cotton bales was shipwrecked off the Wirral, and the bales washed ashore. Wood and parts of the ship soon sank into the sand, but the bales of cotton did not. Then grass started to grow in the cotton bales, and this held firm in the sand. Bales of cotton were then deliberately sunk into the foreshore, and a wall was built on them. They did not sink, and the two lighthouses along this shore were built on the same principle, Leasowe first, then New Brighton in 1827 at a cost of £27,000. Photograph 30413, opposite, shows that the entrance was 40ft up the lighthouse, and could only be reached by climbing up an iron ladder fixed to the outside of the 90ft structure. In the late 1980s the lighthouse was sold, refurbished and subsequently marketed as a quirky site for honeymooners and those wanting something different for a weekend break.

Irby is one of many Scandinavian names on the Wirral, and means 'place of the Irishmen', referring to the Vikings who settled the area, who had previously lived in Ireland.

The last light beamed out across Liverpool Bay from Moreton Lighthouse on the Wirral on 15 July 1908, when the last recorded keeper was a Mrs Williams, the only known woman lighthouse keeper of her time. After a period as a tearoom, the building remained derelict until 1989, when it was restored and converted into an information centre and Ranger office for the North Wirral Coastal Park.

Aintree Racecourse has a long and varied history. The first (flat) race was held there on 7 July 1829. Ten years later, the first Grand National was run. The winning horse, 'Lottery', had to negotiate a stone wall and a stretch of ploughed land as well as the usual fences. The greatest name associated with Aintree is probably the legendary racehorse 'Red Rum'. In addition to his unequalled three wins in the Grand National, he also twice finished second in the race. His achievements were all the more remarkable as he had acquired a debilitating bone disease before his first National win. After his death in 1995 he was buried by the winning post, a fitting honour for the course's much-loved hero.

Motor racing came to Aintree in the 1950s, when the course hosted five British Grand Prix, notably including the first Grand Prix win for Stirling Moss, in 1955.

Ellesmere Port has produced two notable figures in the world of football, whose careers took somewhat similar paths. **Joe Mercer** was born in the town in 1914. After playing for Ellesmere Port FC he moved to Everton, and later Arsenal, winning three Championship medals, and five England caps. After his playing career he went on to great success as a manager, most notably with the League-winning Manchester City team of the late 1960s. **Stan Cullis** was born in the town in 1916. He joined Wolverhampton Wanderers as a teenager, helping them to finish second in the 1937-38 and 1938-39 seasons. He won 12 England caps and later went on to great success as Wolves' manager, leading their great side of the 1950s to three League Championships.

QUIZ QUESTIONS

Answers on page 50.

1. Why is there a monument to Lord Nelson in Exchange Flags Square, behind Liverpool Town Hall, and what do the four chained figures around it represent?

2. How did Liverpool's Bold Street get its name?

3. Statues of which two famous artists stand by the entrance steps of Liverpool's Walker Art Gallery?

4. What is a liver bird, as depicted on Liverpool's Royal Liver Building at Pier Head?

5. What are the Three Graces of Liverpool?

6. Birkenhead Park, which was completed in 1846, was the first park in the country to be provided at public expense. It was designed by someone who was later responsible for a spectacular giant greenhouse - who was he?

7. Where was Liverpool's 'Holy Corner'?

8. What is very special about Birkenhead's Hamilton Square?

9. What unusual feature can be found in the porch of Christ Church at High Bebington, on the Wirral?

10. What was a Wirral Horn?

LIVERPOOL, THE WATERLOO COLUMN 1895 36645

PORT SUNLIGHT, DELL BRIDGE AND THE LYCEUM c1955 P188036

RECIPE

SCOUSE

There are many variations of Scouse, according to family tradition - one of them is given here, but is not claimed to be the definitive recipe!

Ingredients

225g/8oz stewing steak
225g/8oz breast of lamb
1 large onion, cut into large chunks
450g/1lb carrots, cut into slices
2.25kg/5lb potatoes
2 stock cubes - preferably Oxo
2 teaspoonfuls vegetable oil
Worcestershire Sauce
Salt and pepper
Water

Cut the meat into large cubes and fry them in the vegetable oil until lightly browned all over. Transfer the meat to a large saucepan and add the onion chunks, then the sliced carrots. Peel and dice 450g/1lb of the potatoes and place on top of the carrots.

Half fill the saucepan with water, and add the crumbled stock cubes and salt and pepper to taste. Bring to the boil, then reduce heat and simmer gently for about two hours.

Peel and roughly chop the remaining potatoes and add to the pan, with a few dashes of Worcestershire Sauce to taste. Simmer for a further two hours, then serve piping hot.

LIVERPOOL, THE EXCHANGE 1887 20001

NEW BRIGHTON, THE PIER 1900 45166

PARKGATE, LOADING MUSSELS 1939 P255011

RECIPE

FRESH MUSSELS WITH PARSLEY

Photograph P255011, opposite, shows Wirral fishermen at Parkgate loading mussels into jute sacks ready for transportation to the restaurants of Cheshire and Liverpool. Shellfish are still gathered by some locals from the brackish sands to the north of Parkgate, but the commercial trade ceased in the 1950s.

Ingredients

450g/1lb fresh mussels
15g/½oz butter
1 clove of garlic, crushed
1 dessertspoonful chopped fresh parsley

Check the mussels and discard any that are open, as they are not safe to eat. Wash and scrub the remaining mussels. Pull off the beards, and use the back of an old knife to knock off any barnacles.

Put the mussels in a large pan with the other ingredients. Put on the lid, and cook over a high heat, shaking the pan from time to time to ensure that nothing sticks and burns. Cook for only enough time to open the mussel shells, then shake again so that the liquid in the pan gets into the mussels. The whole cooking process should take about five minutes.

Serve the mussels immediately in deep wide bowls with the cooking liquid poured over them, accompanied by crusty bread to mop it up.

QUIZ ANSWERS

1. Although Lord Nelson was a hero all over the country after his victory and death at the Battle of Trafalgar in 1805, he was particularly important to the merchants of Liverpool. His victories over the French navy meant that they were now free to ply their trade throughout the world. The bronze monument, which was funded by public subscription, was unveiled in October 1813, and was Liverpool's first major public sculpture. The inscription on it is Nelson's famous command 'England expects every man to do his duty', and the statues represent sailors taken prisoner at Nelson's four great victories at Cape St Vincent, the Nile, Copenhagen and Trafalgar.

2. Bold Street was named after the Bold family, who owned the land when the street was first laid out in the early 1700s.

3. Raphael and Michelangelo.

4. No-one is exactly sure what the mysterious stone Liver Birds really represent. They may be cormorants or even griffins, but it is generally believed that their name is derived from the 'lyver' seaweed that they grasp in their bills.

5. A group of buildings that is believed by many to be one of the most imposing waterfront views in the world - the Royal Liver Building, the Cunard Building and the Port of Liverpool Building.

6. Birkenhead Park was designed by Joseph Paxton, the famous head gardener of Chatsworth. He was later to be knighted for his design of the Crystal Palace for the Great Exhibition of 1851.

7. The crossroads at the Lord Street end of Church Street was known as 'Holy Corner', because (Our) Lord Street, Church Street, (White) Chapel and Paradise Street met here.

8. Birkenhead's Hamilton Square, which was completed in 1826, has the largest number of Grade 1 listed buildings in England in one place, with the exception of Trafalgar Square in London.

9. A dinosaur footprint, which was found in some sandstone rock from the old Storeton stone quarries. It has been set into the wall of the tower porch of Christ Church.

10. After the Norman Conquest in 1066, the Wirral became a favoured hunting ground for the Norman kings and noblemen. A common sound in the medieval period would have been that of the Wirral Horn, a brass-tipped hunting horn used by the foresters of the peninsula. It is today portrayed in many coats of arms associated with the Wirral which originate from this time.

WALLASEY, MAY COTTAGE AND THE NOOK 1898   W164012

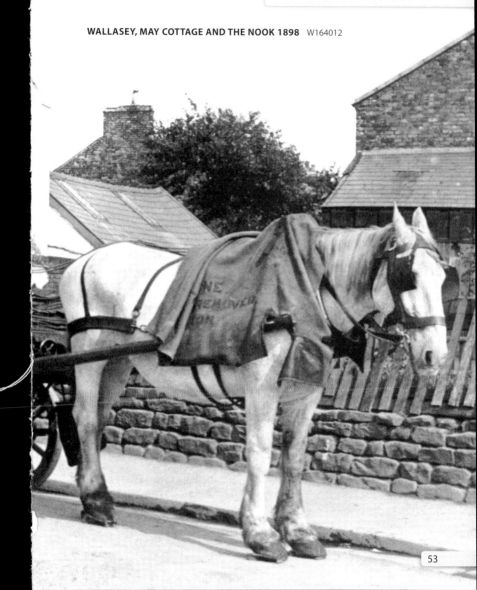

FRANCIS FRITH

PIONEER VICTORIAN PHOTOGRAPHER

Francis Frith, founder of the world-famous photographic archive, was a complex and multi-talented man. A devout Quaker and a highly successful Victorian businessman, he was philosophical by nature and pioneering in outlook. By 1855 he had already established a wholesale grocery business in Liverpool, and sold it for the astonishing sum of £200,000, which is the equivalent today of over £15,000,000. Now in his thirties, and captivated by the new science of photography, Frith set out on a series of pioneering journeys up the Nile and to the Near East.

INTRIGUE AND EXPLORATION

He was the first photographer to venture beyond the sixth cataract of the Nile. Africa was still the mysterious 'Dark Continent', and Stanley and Livingstone's historic meeting was a decade into the future. The conditions for picture taking confound belief. He laboured for hours in his wicker dark-room in the sweltering heat of the desert, while the volatile chemicals fizzed dangerously in their trays. Back in London he exhibited his photographs and was 'rapturously cheered' by members of the Royal Society. His reputation as a photographer was made overnight.

VENTURE OF A LIFE-TIME

By the 1870s the railways had threaded their way across the country, and Bank Holidays and half-day Saturdays had been made obligatory by Act of Parliament. All of a sudden the working man and his family were able to enjoy days out, take holidays, and see a little more of the world.

With typical business acumen, Francis Frith foresaw that these new tourists would enjoy having souvenirs to commemorate their days out. For the next thirty years he travelled the country by train and by pony and trap, producing fine photographs of seaside resorts and beauty spots that were keenly bought by millions of Victorians. These prints were painstakingly pasted into family albums and pored over during the dark nights of winter, rekindling precious memories of summer excursions. Frith's studio was soon supplying retail shops all over the country, and by 1890 F Frith & Co had become the greatest specialist photographic publishing company in the world, with over 2,000 sales outlets, and pioneered the picture postcard.

FRANCIS FRITH'S LEGACY

Francis Frith had died in 1898 at his villa in Cannes, his great project still growing. By 1970 the archive he created contained over a third of a million pictures showing 7,000 British towns and villages.

Frith's legacy to us today is of immense significance and value, for the magnificent archive of evocative photographs he created provides a unique record of change in the cities, towns and villages throughout Britain over a century and more. Frith and his fellow studio photographers revisited locations many times down the years to update their views, compiling for us an enthralling and colourful pageant of British life and character.

We are fortunate that Frith was dedicated to recording the minutiae of everyday life. For it is this sheer wealth of visual data, the painstaking chronicle of changes in dress, transport, street layouts, buildings, housing and landscape that captivates us so much today, offering us a powerful link with the past and with the lives of our ancestors.

Computers have now made it possible for Frith's many thousands of images to be accessed almost instantly. The archive offers every one of us an opportunity to examine the places where we and our families have lived and worked down the years. Its images, depicting our shared past, are now bringing pleasure and enlightenment to millions around the world a century and more after his death.

For further information visit: www.francisfrith.com

INTERIOR DECORATION

Frith's photographs can be seen framed and as giant wall murals in thousands of pubs, restaurants, hotels, banks, retail stores and other public buildings throughout Britain. These provide interesting and attractive décor, generating strong local interest and acting as a powerful reminder of gentler days in our increasingly busy and frenetic world.

FRITH PRODUCTS

All Frith photographs are available as prints and posters in a variety of different sizes and styles. In the UK we also offer a range of other gift and stationery products illustrated with Frith photographs, although many of these are not available for delivery outside the UK – see our web site for more information on the products available for delivery in your country.

THE INTERNET

Over 100,000 photographs of Britain can be viewed and purchased on the Frith web site. The web site also includes memories and reminiscences contributed by our customers, who have personal knowledge of localities and of the people and properties depicted in Frith photographs. If you wish to learn more about a specific town or village you may find these reminiscences fascinating to browse. Why not add your own comments if you think they would be of interest to others? See **www.francisfrith.com**

PLEASE HELP US BRING FRITH'S PHOTOGRAPHS TO LIFE

Our authors do their best to recount the history of the places they write about. They give insights into how particular towns and villages developed, they describe the architecture of streets and buildings, and they discuss the lives of famous people who lived there. But however knowledgeable our authors are, the story they tell is necessarily incomplete.

Frith's photographs are so much more than plain historical documents. They are living proofs of the flow of human life down the generations. They show real people at real moments in history; and each of those people is the son or daughter of someone, the brother or sister, aunt or uncle, grandfather or grandmother of someone else. All of them lived, worked and played in the streets depicted in Frith's photographs.

We would be grateful if you would give us your insights into the places shown in our photographs: the streets and buildings, the shops, businesses and industries. Post your memories of life in those streets on the Frith website: what it was like growing up there, who ran the local shop and what shopping was like years ago; if your workplace is shown tell us about your working day and what the building is used for now. Read other visitors' memories and reconnect with your shared local history and heritage. With your help more and more Frith photographs can be brought to life, and vital memories preserved for posterity, and for the benefit of historians in the future.

Wherever possible, we will try to include some of your comments in future editions of our books. Moreover, if you spot errors in dates, titles or other facts, please let us know, because our archive records are not always completely accurate—they rely on 140 years of human endeavour and hand-compiled records. You can email us using the contact form on the website.

Thank you!

For further information, trade, or author enquiries please contact us at the address below:

The Francis Frith Collection, Frith's Barn, Teffont, Salisbury, Wiltshire, England SP3 5QP.

Tel: +44 (0)1722 716 376 Fax: +44 (0)1722 716 881
e-mail: sales@francisfrith.co.uk **www.francisfrith.com**